Prison Segmentation For Exit Contracts

Concept

Rev. Mike Wanner

Table Of Contents

Introduction

I invite every reader to consider the ideas that can create freedom for taxpayers from the extreme costs of imprisoning vast numbers of our fellow citizens. We have taken for granted that we somehow can afford these prices.

Alas and unfortunately, the costs of incarceration are about to eat up the quality of the American Dream. We are all gradually being banished to involuntary servitude by our insecurities.

Yes, we are threatened by great evil in the world. There is no need for us to overreact. There is some justification for the restrictions that are imposed upon those who have been convicted of a crime.

As taxpayers, we in the greater community have an interest in how our tax dollars are spent. Incarceration is a considerable expense, and if there were unlimited funds in our national budget, there would be no need to consider changing anything unless some additional fairness was a prominent goal.

Unfortunately, the national budget is stretched by government expenditures, and it may make sense for us to evaluate the reasonableness of our expenses. We could find there are little opportunities for relaxation until change happens.

We could find that there are options not yet considered. This book is an invitation to look at what we are doing related to incarceration and see what we find.

1 - What Is an Exit Contract

With this writing, I am proposing some ideas to prepare for the exit of prisoners by starting something that can help:

1. The Prisoners be ready for release.

2. The Prisons be in agreement with their overseers.

3. Businesses to find new ideas for projects that can work.

4. The prisoner to have the needed time and access to prepare for an eventual nest from which one can create a full life.

This proposal lays out a plan that can be manipulated to the satisfaction of all. The strength and flexibility come from the voluntary structure which brings excellent freedom of thought.

I continue to start discussions about little things that could make a difference in the systems and invite you to dialogue with me along the way.

If we can arrange opportunities for people, freedom can blossom for those who are ready and deserving.

The Contract could have:
1. A Part of the Prison for Readiness where the contractor and the prisoners design the project.
2. A Part where the contract initiator provides the site and work to be accomplished.
3. The performance periods and tasks.

2 - Why I am Writing This Book

I want to trigger mindset shifts in the prisoners as well as employees and the community. We need a lot more Objective Productive Dialogues about Enhancing the lives of Prison Employees, Prisoners, Taxpayers and the Families of Each of these groups.

I hope that this book continues the work started by my other books and continues to enhance the lives of Prison Employees, Prisoners, Taxpayers and the Families of Each of these groups?

As I have been writing my early books on the subject of Prisons, the complexity of the process has been amazing to me.

The books that I have previously published so far about the prison situations are:

1. *Angel Raphael Speaks Volume 4: Angels, Addicts, Alcoholics & Prisoners - Oh Yeah!*
2. *Angel Raphael Speaks Volume 5: Prisoners Caring for Alcoholics - Australia In Miniature   Projects Intro*
3. *Angel Raphael Speaks Volume 6: Prisoners Caring for Addicts - Australia In Miniature For   Addicts*
4. *Prison Jobs Now: Providing Care For Addicts And Alcoholics*
5. *Angel Raphael Speaks - Prisons (A Kindle only book -2013)*
6. *Contained Care Communities: Concept*
7. *Australia In Miniature*
8. *Prison Possibilities Dialogue Series: Concept*
9. *Prison Possibilities Dialogue Series: Volume 2 Dialogues*
10. *Prison Possibilities Dialogue Series: Volume 3 Dialogues*
11. *Prison Possibilities Dialogue Series: Volume 4 Dialogues*
12. *Prison Possibilities Dialogue Series: Volume 5 Dialogues*

3 - Prisoner Profiles

In *Prison Possibilities Dialogue Series: Volume 3 Dialogues,* I proposed a business enterprise be created to write, post and share prisoner profiles so that people outside the prison system could shop for skills that prisoners within the system already had.

That type of service could be particularly useful for businesses who needed to access talent but lacked the resources to hire from the available community of skill holders. Additionally, the pool of talent may make potential projects possible that would not be otherwise justifiable.

I will post Dialogue 26 "Prison Profile Bureaus" from *Prison Possibilities Dialogue Series: Volume 3 Dialogues* in the next Chapter. Other references to Dialogues will also be excerpts from parts of the series.

1st Style Brief Prisoner Profile

In the early stages, a Brief Prisoner Profile should be enough to get the conversation started. My suggestion would focus on the word brief as communication can be difficult and there is excellent value in precise information that can fairly portray the history and capabilities of an individual. Success will be enhanced by appropriate wordsmithing to be efficient and fair so a lot of people can be screened efficiently and many will have additional opportunities they otherwise may not have.

I would recommend a single page for a brief profile that is visually similar to and as concise as a Dialogue format from the dialogue Series.

The Dialogue format is a single Page Configuration <220 Words, in a 6 x9 book format with all .5 margins, Title Font 20 Pt. Times New Roman, Body Font 14 Pt. Times New Roman. Adherence to the desired form will go a long way to simplify the process. Thank You.

A clear example will be added below the 2nd Style.

2nd Style Prisoner Profile - Bureau Style

Prisoner profile formats could vary from bureau to bureau and format as much detail as the requestor wants and could include:

1. Credit Report

2. Educational Report

3. Criminal Record

4. Skills and Certifications

5. Family History and obligations

6. Children and spouses

7. Prisoner performance during incarceration

8. History of Any Violence

Format -Brief Prisoner Profile
For_____

Present Location_____

E-mail address for further info_____

Birthplace_____ Birthdate_____

Marital Status _____Children_____

Upon discharge, I plan to live at_____

with_____

Or I am open to relocate_____

I am scheduled to be released _____

_____

I was convicted of _____

I ___may or ____may not be eligible for earlier release.

My Education includes _____

_____

My skills include_____

_____

_____

_____

I have trade skills in_____

_____

I would really enjoy doing_____

_____

Special Aptitudes include_____

_____

Special Notes_____

_____

Prepared by _____Tel._____

E-Mail_____Web_____

4 - "Prisoner Profile Bureaus
[Dialogue 26]

A New Business Opportunity may be to create a Prisoner Profile Bureau if that is legal and proper to do so. Check out the legality first.

The idea is that many prisoners could benefit from the availability of a publicly available profile on as many aspects of their life as makes sense for potential employers. What kind of products to create and who should pay for them are not my focus now, but the value of such a service could be significant.

This idea will only be successful if the orchestrator of the process has sufficient credibility to present themselves to the public as an objective credible resource. My thinking is that this could be a sideline for credit bureaus or it could be a government service or government subsidized service to increase the likelihood that those discharged can stay out. Family status could help to show that the one discharged has the motivation to do a good and credible job.

Skills and capabilities and certifications can help to target an audience for the bureau and increase the value of profiles for the one discharged. The intent of the service would be to qualify great candidates for great companies so that the prisoner can find a remarkable job and the employer a long-lasting employee. In that process, the community can have more productivity, fewer prisoners, more workers and fewer prison costs."

12

5 - Prison Rehabilitation Limitations

The Title of this chapter and content to follow comes directly from Angel Raphael Speaks Message Set 10 because it sets the stage for the reasoning behind part of the exit idea. I swap my content in and out because I do not expect readers to read all my books in order to follow the concepts and understand what I am saying about a particular facet that I am writing about at the moment.

"Prison Rehabilitation

The answer to prison rehabilitation is prisoner purpose. While some institutions may have initiated programs to engage their residents, the feeling of a purposeful life brings a new reality to the incarcerated.

The purposes, to consider, are the ones that work for the incarcerated as well as the society which actually pays the bills. Individual characteristics to include would be the creation of a feeling of accomplishment generated by prisoner effort and drastic cost savings for the institution.

The real loss of prisons is wasted time, no productivity and no graciousness of interactive genius. If invited, the right use of time can provide different results than now seen....

…The best way to learn about what is possible is to listen to the troubled stories of the incarcerated people. Their genius can be tapped by mining information about how to fill the gap that they slipped in to so that newer walkers on their path can find it filled by their charity of sharing their pain as a love patch to the sinkholes of society.

The answers through this channel are coming differently than most could conceive and that is because neither you nor I have a job whose agenda has its own needs…

…Their opportunities are paramount in the areas of personal safety for all and the possibility to create new meaningful arrangements that are self-sustaining at all levels of the resident base and those employed in the industry. " ARS 10

14

6 - A Brief on A New Path

Like all my books about prison, this one will be deliberately brief for a number of reasons. The intensity of the ideas and thought streams that are coming to me will serve best if they can be integrated and there needs to be enough space to combine and separate concepts so they can be comprehended.

Moving too fast will be problematic and shift to a complexity that does not serve anybody. Clarity is the goal, and that is enhanced when the concept being considered is large enough to focus on but also small enough not to be lost in the process.

A large part of the complexity of prisons is analogous to a tree, where eventually everything matters. When you have a sick branch, the tree will be ultimately affected.

When you have a sick tree, the branches can be impacted much quicker because the nutrients for each flow through the tree to reach them. (This concept is shared for conceptualization only as I have no forestry experience, but you can let me know if I am wrong. No worries.)

The foundation, using a house analogy, supports the walls that support the floor above and then the walls above progressively until the roof is finished but then we need to put on a roof so that everything below is protected down to the foundation.

I have shared the tree trunk above and will bring up some example branches in the following chapters, but then you will add more and more so the Idea of Exile Possibilities blossoms.

15

7 - "Prisoners Can Contribute and Evolve"
[Dialogue 1]

"Each facility has different rules about the rights and movements of Prisoners. I would encourage each prisoner to consider participation to the full extent of their interest, ability, and freedom.

Knowing the rules is an essential part of all things in which a person participates. Patience will serve prisoners well if they wait until the time that comments are invited and to what degree participation is unmoderated.

Please know that prison staffs can be flexible like anybody else when the people they are interacting with act in a more peaceful way. I invite you to be aware of the way that others may perceive you.

Human nature is to reciprocate appropriately so that respectful behavior is reciprocated with polite behavior. I invite you to realize that respect for others can serve you well over time.

Please pay attention and see what you can do that will make a difference in small ways. Little changes can add up over time and create new options for all participants.

I have been amazed at the fact that almost always someone will notice changes and ask why. Why leads to further conversation and further understanding and the expansion of possibilities." This dialogue reference and the one that follows are from my books in the *Prison Possibilities Dialogue Series*."

8 - "What Rights Would a Prisoner Be Willing To Trade for What Benefits?

[Dialogue 2]

Prisoners have rights that are protected by the U. S. Constitution. Do you know all your rights? If you have someone dear in prison or jail, you may benefit them by learning what their rights are. There are even some rights before jail. Inmates have some rights to be free, from inhuman conditions that may be seen as "cruel and unusual" punishment.

The laws are old and complicated, and I am not qualified to interpret them but therein I think may lie some need for updating or modernization. Yes, it seems that the Americans with Disabilities Act does apply but also some highly restrictive narrow rules. Yes, they are entitled to adequate medical care too.

And the list goes on but the questions I ask is what laws could be changed to allow prisoners to waive rights permanently.

Releasing institutions from compliance with the law are not allowed but changing rules to allow institutional freedom could allow prisoners to surrender their rights and prisons to save money and taxpayers to be taxed less.

The question flows from the original Angel Raphael Speaks Message series.

"Prisoner Surrender of Rights

Those interested in any of the concepts shared could also consider surrendering of some rights to further the benefits to the governmental unit. ARS11"

17

9 - "My Ideas Are Seeds; You Can Be A Farmer
[Dialogue 4]

Reasonable people can assess reality and decide for themselves what might be possible if we avoid all the old structure and streamline the process of creating reasonable options to what we are doing. We are not locked into the realities of yesterday.

Common Sense is not so common anymore, and I invite all readers to start dialogues that are reasonable, revolutionary, realistic and pursue-able. Why not have a little coffee meeting and talk about simple steps to finding freedom for someone by changing rules that affect many?

I would encourage efforts that are Pro-Bono for the greater good as I expect they can be more productive on a shorter timeline than trying to free a specific person for jaywalking.

A broad brush is excellent for painting the side of a barn, but the effort here is to dot I's and cross T's in a legal document that sets many people free with reasonable rules that change criteria.

The right balance is what you would be wise to pursue, but purpose, patience, persistence, politicking, and people will be the keys which can open doors for many others. Furthermore, acceleration is furthered by respect for all involved at every level. People are not required to listen to new ideas but usually will if they are objectively and respectfully presented."

Disclaimer

I, the author, am not involved with prisons or prisoners but am sharing what is coming to me in an effort to spread understanding and trigger conversation that can be helpful. This book is not directed at any one prison or any series of prisons because they may all be very different.

There are about 6,000 incarceration facilities in America alone the messages here could be off a bit when the words are taken literally. The hope is that the conversation triggered will be helpful to all involved in the system.

There can be a lot of topics that need further development, and if you see any, I Invite feedback and concept proposals. It will take a considerable amount of information to develop all the potentials that come up.

10 - A Contract Plan

A contract is an agreement between two parties, and in this case, there will be the prisoner and the business owner who prepared the document. The process provides an opportunity for both. Careful attention is needed to deliver the jobs without taking away jobs from the broader community where there is also a great need.

But how can that be done? Creativity will be needed, but I believe there will be an opportunity if we all get to thinking and break through to new levels of reasonable options.

The old business concept of building a better mousetrap can still be an image that spurs one on to the creative genius that lies within. In reality, none of this will be easy but the work of a butterfly to exit a cocoon is not easy either but the struggle to transform is worthy of the effort.

The challenge of this concept can be visualized by developing an idea like the one from Angel Raphael Speaks Volume 4 which lays down the opportunity for prisoners that is scrutinized and supervised for a time and provides workers with an On-the-Job Training Dynamic that can lead to credentials that can lead to employment at the end.

The 1st Development segment could be within the prison and lead to a detailed contract, and some sort of Business orchestrated workplace and residence that can host the employment contracted for. This segment will likely be brief.

11 - Work & Housing Plan & Backup

After part One, the next item on the agenda is the setup for work and housing is to design and arrange for the space needed. Consideration is also required for rules that would determine how space will be used and who will have access and the house rules.

The situations for prisoners could vary significantly by the employer designing the contract, the skills of the prisoners, the task at hand and the level of freedom that will be afforded by the agreement.

A determination of all rights and privileges needs to be itemized and it would be helpful to include specific language to declare general rules that will apply if there is an unaddressed area (i.e., Perhaps something like, Additional freedoms are not granted unless the representative of the contract designers allows an exception on a case by case basis.)

A formal authority plan should be specified, and a backup plan should be in place in case there is a disruption of the agreement and progress of the project. A cancellation timeline, consequences, and specific performance settings declaration should also be in place.

12 - Family & Social Considerations & Backup

A motivator for many prisoners entering segmentation may be the ability to see and spend time with family. While segmentation may help with that, it is essential that every bit of access and any restrictions are explicitly laid out in the contract referenced above.

It may be that a segment for visitation and another for exit contracts are less than compatible so details are essential and caution is advised.

Families can be delightful in many circumstances but sometimes historical conflicts can be retriggered and might cause a prisoner to act in ways that they probably would not without that triggering. It may be better to have an issue of retriggering happen before discharge where it can all be worked out before the release and a potential recidivism event.

An emotional outburst from a family member may lead to a cancellation of the motivation and turn a good idea into a mess, so it is essential that circumstances like that are avoided.

A plan B is needed, so the ex-prisoner has an option to fall back on in case something does not go as planned. Plan B could be as simple as starting over with a revised set of goals and contractual obligations or general population again until things settle down and a new idea emerges.

13 - Food Plan & Backup

The next item on the agenda for someone helping set up for a prisoner exit contract is to design and set a location for the prisoner to eat regularly. As you see in the title, it is just not good enough for a prisoner to expect to have a family member feed them once they are moved in but better to plan it.

Every day the prisoner will need to eat, and that will need to be preplanned. Three meals plus snacks plus beverages.

In addition to what is planned and included in the contract, Forbidden substances need to be explicitly identified and kept away from the prisoner/candidate.

An emotional outburst from a family member and a cancellation of a food service arrangement may lead to panic, trouble, and other reactive behavior.

A plan B is needed, so the ex-prisoner has an option to fall back on in case something does not go as planned.

14 - Job Plan & Backup

The Last item on the agenda is the details of the job plan.

The contract proposer should provide all the details with specificity:

Specifications:

_____

Quantity:

_____

Any certifications needed:

_____

Compensation Details:

_____

Plan B (In case something does not go as planned.)

_____

For
Considering
These
Ideas

Ever

It Does Not Help Prayer Still Does!

17 - Resource List

Distant Healing Sessions (or Join Mail List) – Write To mikewann@voicenet.com

Books by Rev. Mike at <u>www.Amazon.com:</u>

Veterans Healing Six Pack
1. *Trauma Healing Options for VA Hospitals: Help for Veterans to Own Their Healing and their future.*
2. *Trauma Healing Action Steps for Veterans: Help to Start Healing*
3. *Trauma Healing Action Steps for Veterans: Empowerment*
4. *Trauma Healing Action Steps for Veterans: Forgiveness*
5. *Trauma Healing Action Steps for Veterans: Thought Freedom*
6. *Tea For Veterans: Welcome One Home*

PTSD Power Pack:
1. *The PTSD Project: Turn Pain To Power*
2. *PTSD & Soul Retrieval: Putting One Back Together*
3. *PTSD & The Purple PAD: Calling all Scientists and PTSD Patients*

Angel Raphael Speaks Volume 1: Take Courage! God Has Healing in Store for You!
Angel Raphael Speaks Volume 2: Take Courage! God Has Healing in Store for You!
Angel Raphael Speaks Volume 3: Take Courage! God Has Healing in Store for You!
Angel Raphael Speaks Volume 4: Angels, Addicts, Alcoholics & Prisoners – Oh Yeah!
Angel Raphael Speaks Volume 5: Prisoners Caring for Alcoholics - Australia In Miniature Projects Intro
Angel Raphael Speaks Volume 6: Prisoners Caring for Addicts - Australia In Miniature For Addicts
Reiki Journaling from Japan
Reiki Is Alive: God's Great Gift
Four Parts to Healing

Prison Cell Clearing & Blessing: Clear Entities, Chase Ghosts, & Create Sacred Space
Prisoner Professors: Show You Are Aware Create Change With Care
Prison Reiki? Maybe Someday? A Gateway To Help Heal Prisons & America?
Judges and An Angel Rule On Possibilities: We Can Cut Sentences & Prison Costs
Ideas For Prison Wardens: Leadership Is Not Easy
Solitary Community: Could Community Support Cut Costs and Issues?
Prison Project Communications Team: Communications Can Change Lives
Motivating & Empowering Prisoners? Invite Prisoners To Find Their Motivation
Prison Segmentation For Safety, And Sanity, Security, Peace, and Space
Prison Segmentation For Security
Dowsing for Prisoners; Answers from Above
Ex-Prisoner Possibilities With Real Estate Investors
Prison Segmentation For Joint Ventures
Prison Segmentation For Your Rehabilitation: R U Ready?
Prison Segmentation For Family Villages
Prison Segmentation For Senior Prisoners
Prison Segmentation For Coaching Clubs
Prison Segmentation For Miracles

Little Books on Kindle.com by Rev. Mike:
English Medical History Questionnaire For Non-English Speakers
English Language Helper For Non-English Speakers
Wise Wonderful Women Are The Well Of The Family
Answers for Test & Research: Dowsing Power
Crisis? Reiki! Baby? Reiki!
Bible References For Healing
Angel Raphael Speaks – Prisons
Angel Raphael Speaks – Veterans
The Saint Off Interstate 95

Angel Raphael Speaks through Rev. Mike Wanner.
Please visit http://www.AngelRaphaelSpeaks.com

18 - Angels Please Prayers

Addict's

Angels of Healing Selected
Help Me to Stay Directed
Come To Me From The Sky
I Am Ready to Succeed Not Try
If I Don't Invite You In
I Might Not Win
I Have Been Lost For Too Long
Help Me To Stay Strong

&

Alcoholic's

Angels of Healing On High
Help Me to Stay Dry
Come To Me From The Sky
I Am Ready to Succeed Not Try
If I Don't Invite You In
I Might Not Win
I Have Been Lost For Too Long
Help Me To Stay Strong

From

http://AngelRaphaelSpeaks.com/AAAAAAA/

19 - Private Channeling

Angel Raphael Speaks a series of free messages that are channeled through Reverend Mike Wanner for the Highest good and Highest Healing of all concerned.

Many questions arise about Reverend Mike doing private channeling, and he does help with that so e-mail him.

Reverend Mike is available worldwide as a psychic channel, emotional release facilitator, spiritual energy practitioner & teacher, and public speaker. He looks forward to meeting you soon!

Email - mikewann@voicenet.com 215-342-1270

PRIVATE SPIRITUAL READINGS/channelings or Spiritual Healing Sessions: Telephone or in person. Rev. Mike is available for individual, intuitive one-on-one sessions with you, his Guide Family, and your Guides. He helps by offering clarity on emotional situations about your life, your purpose, your spirituality, and the release of stuffed emotions and cellular memory.

Connect to the love of your Guides today!
Contact Rev. Mike for an appointment.

Sessions available:

Spiritual Readings
Angel Channeling
Distant Reiki Healing
Distant Clearing of Stuffed Emotions
Distant Clearing Cellular Memory
Distant Clearing Energy Blockages
Distant Clearing of the Chakras
Customized needs
Mastermind dowsing responses to yes/no direction finding questions.

Rev. Mike is a facilitator of healing. He brings you and the Divine together so that you can align with the Divine and have a great time and a great life. All healing is between you and God, as it should be. Go ahead and start without Rev. Mike. Visit his prayer site http://www.Create-A-Prayer.com. Take the first step NOW.

20 - Reverend Mike Wanner

Rev. Mike Wanner started his metaphysical and ministerial studies with Reiki in 1993 and had studied seven styles of Reiki in the U.S., Japan, Canada, Denmark and Australia. He is certified to teach. He became certified to teach Integrated Energy Therapy in 1999 and co-taught the first IET class of the new Millennium. Mike began dowsing in 2001.

Ordained as a Metaphysical Minister of the International Metaphysical Ministry and an Interfaith Minister of the Circle of Miracles Ministry, Rev. Mike practices and teaches spiritual energy therapies in the Philadelphia Area.

Rev. Mike holds ministerial degrees from the University of Metaphysics and the University of Sedona. He is a Pastoral Care Associate at Jefferson - Aria - Frankford Hospital. He taught at the National Academy of Massage Therapy and Health Sciences.

Rev. Mike was a faculty member of the Medical Mission Sister's Center for Human Integration's School of Integrated Body/Mind Therapies in Fox Chase, Philadelphia, PA for twelve years.

Rev. Mike is licensed by the teaching of Intuitional Metaphysics to practice Spiritual Healing and Scientific Prayer. Mike is also a Prayer therapist.

Rev. Mike was elected in 2007 to the status of "Fellow of the American Institute of Stress."

In 2008, Rev. Mike became a practitioner of Coincidental Recognition as he incorporated the CoRe system into his spiritual healing practice.

In 2009, Rev. Mike trademarked a new healing process called Quantum Quatro! Subtle Energy System Support®.
In 2011, Rev. Mike joined the outreach program known as the Health Advantage Group.

In 2012, Rev. Mike became a Certified Professional Coach by The Master Coaching Academy and Joined The Personal Empowerment Group.

Prior to his spiritual, ministerial and coaching studies, Rev. Mike worked for Sears Roebuck and Co. while in High School and after graduation, until he joined the U. S. Air Force in 1965. He returned to Sears from Vietnam in 1969 and stayed until 1978. His final Sears assignment was as an efficiency expert in Methods - Operational Research and Development.

He volunteered with Burholme Emergency Medical Services from 1969 and is still a Life Member and Board of Directors Member. He started a private ambulance company in 1975 and worked professionally in the field until 2001 when he devoted his full attention to real estate investing, healing, coaching, and writing.

www.ReverendMikeWanner.com

www.ingramcontent.com/pod-product-compliance
Lightning Source LLC
Chambersburg PA
CBHW071202220526
45468CB00003B/1125